MW00977446

One-Skein
(or less!) Projects

With a single skein of yarn or scraps from your stash, you can crochet lots of fun little gifts and fund-raising items (especially in team colors!). Bonus online technique videos make our clear instructions extra easy.

2

6

8

11

14

16

19

22

24

26

28

31

36

39

LEISURE ARTS, INC. • Maumelle, Arkansas

Headband

▮▮▮▯▭ EASY

Finished Size: Approximately 18" (45.5 cm) circumference

SHOPPING LIST

Yarn (Medium Weight)

☐ Orange - 30 yards (27.5 meters)

☐ Teal - 13 yards (12 meters)

Crochet Hook

☐ Size H (5 mm)

GAUGE INFORMATION

Gauge Swatch: 3" (7.5 cm) diameter

Work same as Motif Rnd 1, page 4

—— STITCH GUIDE ——

TREBLE CROCHET

(abbreviated tr)

YO twice, insert hook in sp indicated, YO and pull up a loop (4 loops on hook), (YO and draw through 2 loops on hook) 3 times.

2-TR CLUSTER (uses one sp)

★ YO twice, insert hook in sp indicated, YO and pull up a loop, (YO and draw through 2 loops on hook) twice; repeat from ★ once **more**, YO and draw through all 3 loops on hook.

BACK POST SINGLE CROCHET

(abbreviated BPsc)

Insert hook from **back** to **front** around post of st indicated *(Fig. 3, page 45)*, YO and pull up a loop, YO and draw through both loops on hook.

INSTRUCTIONS
Motif

Rnd 1 (Right side)**:** With Teal and using an adjustable loop *(Figs. 1a-d, page 44)*, ch 3, tr in ring **(counts as first 2-tr Cluster)**, ch 4, (work 2-tr Cluster in ring, ch 4) 7 times; join with slip st to top of first 2-tr Cluster: 8 ch-4 sps.

Note: Loop a short piece of yarn around any stitch to mark Rnd 1 as **right** side.

Rnd 2: Ch 1, (sc, hdc, 3 dc, hdc, sc) in next ch-4 sp and in each ch-4 sp around; join with slip st to first sc, finish off: 8 Petals.

Rnd 3: With **right** side facing and working **behind** Petals, join Orange with slip st in top of any 2-tr Cluster on Rnd 1, ch 1; work BPsc around same Cluster, ch 7, (work BPsc around next 2-tr Cluster, ch 7) around; join with slip st to first BPsc: 8 ch-7 sps.

Rnd 4: Ch 1, (sc, hdc, 2 dc, 3 tr, 2 dc, hdc, sc) in first ch-7 sp and in each ch-7 sp around; join with slip st to first sc, finish off: 8 Petals.

First Band

Row 1: With **right** side facing, join Orange with slip st ▓ in sp before first sc of any Petal *(Fig. 4, page 46)*; ch 60, being careful **not** to twist ch, skip next 3 Petals, slip st in sp **before** first sc of next Petal, ch 1, **turn**; sc in each ch across, slip st in same sp as joining slip st, finish off.

Second Band

Row 1: With **right** side facing, skip next Petal from second slip st of First Band and join Orange with slip st in sp **before** first sc of next Petal; ch 60, being careful **not** to twist ch, skip next 3 Petals, slip st in sp **before** first sc of next Petal, ch 1, **turn**; sc in each ch across, slip st in same sp as joining slip st, finish off.

Curly-Q Hair Ornament

EASY

SHOPPING LIST

Yarn (Medium Weight) MEDIUM 4

- ☐ 15 yards (13.5 meters) **each** color

Crochet Hook

- ☐ Size H (5 mm)

Additional Supplies

- ☐ Hairband - 2½" (6.5 cm) diameter

INSTRUCTIONS

First Section

Row 1: Working around band, join first color with sc ***(see Joining with Sc, page 43)***; work 5 sc around band: 6 sc.

Row 2: Ch 14, turn; 2 sc in second ch from hook and in each ch across; slip st in first 2 sc on band, ★ † ch 14, turn; 2 sc in second ch from hook and in each ch across, slip st in same sc on band as last slip st †, slip st in next sc; repeat from ★ 3 times **more**, then repeat from † to † once; finish off: 5 Curly-Qs.

Second Section

Row 1: Join next color with slip st in same sc as last slip st on First Section; work 6 sc around band.

Row 2: Ch 14, turn; 2 sc in second ch from hook and in each ch across; slip st in first 2 sc on band, ★ † ch 14, turn; 2 sc in second ch from hook and in each ch across, slip st in same sc on band as last slip st †, slip st in next sc; repeat from ★ 3 times **more**, then repeat from † to † once; finish off: 5 Curly-Qs.

Optional Third Section: Work Second Section once **more**, joining third color in same sc as last slip st on Second Section.

 Coffee Cuff

 EASY

Finished Size: 9¾" circumference x 2¾" tall (25 cm x 7 cm)

SHOPPING LIST

Yarn (Medium Weight) [MEDIUM 4]

- ☐ Navy - 20 yards (18.5 meters)
- ☐ Gold - 6 yards (5.5 meters)
- ☐ White - 3 yards (2.5 meters)
- ☐ Red - small amount

Crochet Hook

- ☐ Size H (5 mm)

  or size needed for gauge

Additional Supplies

- ☐ Yarn needle

GAUGE INFORMATION

13 sc and 16 rows = 4" (10 cm)

Gauge Swatch: 4" wide x 2" high
(10 cm x 5 cm)

With Navy, ch 14.

Row 1: Sc in second ch from hook and in each ch across: 13 sc.

Rows 2-8: Ch 1, turn; sc in each sc across.

Finish off.

INSTRUCTIONS

With Navy, ch 31.

Row 1 (Right side): Sc in second ch from hook and in each ch across: 30 sc.

Note: Loop a short piece of yarn around any stitch to mark Row 1 as **right** side.

Row 2: Ch 1, turn; sc in each sc across.

Row 3: Ch 1, turn; sc in each sc across ▣ changing to Gold in last sc made *(Fig. 6a, page 46)*; do **not** cut Navy.

Row 4: Ch 1, turn; sc in each sc across.

Row 5: Ch 1, turn; sc in each sc across changing to Navy in last sc made; cut Gold

Row 6: Ch 1, turn; sc in each sc across changing to White in last sc made; do not cut Navy

Row 7: Ch 1, turn; sc in each sc across.

Row 8: Ch 1, turn; sc in each sc across changing to Navy in last sc made; cut White.

Rows 9-11: Ch 1, turn; sc in each sc across; at end of Row 11, do **not** finish off.

Edging: Ch 1, do **not** turn; working in ends of rows, sc in each row across; finish off.

Opposite End Edging: With **right** side facing and working in ends of rows across opposite edge, ▣ join Navy with sc in first row *(see Joining With Sc, page 43)*; sc in each row across; finish off leaving a long end for sewing.

Vertical Stripe Accents: Using Red, Gold, or White, make a slip knot. With **right** side facing, holding slip knot and working yarn on **wrong** side of piece, insert hook in beginning ch and ▣ pull loop of slip knot through st, working from bottom edge to top edge, (slip st around sc on next row) across; finish off.

Randomly space 4 more Vertical Stripe Accents.

Thread yarn needle with long end and working through **both** loops of each st, ▣ whipstitch ends together *(Fig. 7, page 47)*; then work a White Vertical Stripe Accent over the seam.

Pincushion

Shown on page 13.

◖◼◼◻◗ **EASY**

Finished Size: Approximately 5" (12.5 cm)
from straight edge to straight edge

SHOPPING LIST

Yarn (Medium Weight) 🧶**4**

☐ Dk Rose - 16 yards (14.5 meters)

☐ Rose - 14 yards (13 meters)

☐ Pink - 12 yards (11 meters)

Crochet Hook

☐ Size H (5 mm)

Additional Supplies

☐ Fabric for cushion

☐ Polyester fiberfill

☐ Sewing needle and thread

INSTRUCTIONS
Front

With Dk Rose, ch 5; join with slip st to form a ring.

Rnd 1 (Right side)**:** Ch 3 **(counts as first dc, now and throughout),** 11 dc in ring; join with slip st to first dc 🎥 changing to Rose *(Fig. 6b, page 46)*, cut Dk Rose: 12 dc.

Note: Loop a short piece of yarn around any stitch to mark Rnd 1 as **right** side.

Rnd 2: Ch 3, 3 dc in next dc, (dc in next dc, 3 dc in next dc) around; join with slip st to first dc changing to Pink, do **not** cut Dk Rose: 24 dc.

Rnd 3: Ch 1, sc in same st, ch 1, skip next dc, (sc, ch 1) twice in next dc, skip next dc, ★ sc in next dc, ch 1, skip next dc, (sc, ch 1) twice in next dc, skip next dc; repeat from ★ around; join with slip st to first sc changing to Rose, cut Pink: 18 sc and 18 ch-1 sps.

Rnd 4: Ch 3, dc in next ch-1 sp and in next sc, 3 dc in next ch-1 sp, dc in next sc and in next ch-1 sp, ★ dc in next sc, dc in next ch-1 sp and in next sc, 3 dc in next ch-1 sp, dc in next sc and in next ch-1 sp; repeat from ★ around; join with slip st to first dc changing to Dk Rose, cut Rose: 48 dc.

Rnd 5: Ch 1, sc in same st, ch 1, skip next dc, sc in next dc, ch 1, skip next dc, (sc, ch 1) twice in next dc, ★ skip next dc, (sc in next dc, ch 1, skip next dc) 3 times, (sc, ch 1) twice in next dc; repeat from ★ around to last 3 dc, skip next dc, sc in next dc, ch 1, skip last dc; join with slip st to first sc, finish off.

Using Front as a guide, cut 2 pieces of fabric, ½" (12 mm) larger on all sides for cushion. With right sides together, sew pieces together using an ½" (12 mm) seam and leaving a 1" (2.5 cm) opening. Turn cushion right side out, stuff firmly with fiberfill, and sew opening closed.

Back

Work same as Front in following color sequence: One rnd **each** of Pink, Dk Rose, Rose, Pink, Dk Rose; at end of Rnd 5, do **not** finish off.

Joining Rnd: With **wrong** sides together and  working through **both** loops of each st on **both** pieces, slip st in each st around, inserting cushion before closing; join with slip st to joining slip st, finish off.

See how different the same pattern looks when you change the color placement.

Bangle Bracelets

  EASY

SHOPPING LIST

Yarn (Medium Weight)

Spiral
- ☐ 14 yards (13 meters)

Ruffled
- ☐ 24 yards (22 meters)

Two Tone
- ☐ Dk Pink -14 yards (13 meters)
- ☐ Pink - 4 yards (3.5 meters)

Crochet Hook
- ☐ Size H (5 mm)

Additional Supplies
- ☐ Bracelets - 3

INSTRUCTIONS
Spiral

Rnd 1: 📹 Join yarn with sc around bracelet *(see Joining With Sc, page 43)*; sc around bracelet until it is filled; twist sts around bracelet in a spiral; join with slip st to first sc, finish off.

Ruffled

Rnd 1: Join yarn with sc around bracelet; sc around bracelet until it is filled; being careful **not** to twist sts, join with slip st to first sc.

Rnd 2: Ch 1, sc in same st, ch 3, (sc in next sc, ch 3) around; join with slip st to first sc, finish off.

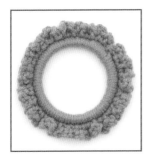

Two Tone

Rnd 1: Join Dk Pink with sc around bracelet; sc around bracelet until it is filled; being careful **not** to twist sts, join with slip st to first sc, finish off.

Rnd 2: Make a slip knot with Pink, holding slip knot and working yarn **beneath** piece, insert hook in any sc,  pull loop of slip knot through st; slip st in each sc around; join with slip st to first slip st, finish off.

Crown

SHOPPING LIST

Yarn (Medium Weight)

☐ 25{35} yards/23{32} meters

Crochet Hook

☐ Size H (5 mm)

or size need for gauge

SIZE INFORMATION

Sizes: Small {Large}

Finished Size:

16{19¼}" /40.5{49} cm

circumference

Size Note: We have printed the instructions for the sizes in different colors to make it easier for you to find:

- Size Small in Blue
- Size Large in Green

Instructions in Black apply to both sizes.

GAUGE INFORMATION

15 dc and 8 rows = 4" (10 cm)

Gauge Swatch: 4" wide x 2" high

(10 cm x 5 cm)

Ch 17.

Row 1: Dc in fourth ch from hook **(3 skipped chs count as first dc)** and in each ch across: 15 dc.

Rows 2-4: Ch 3 **(counts as first dc)**, turn; dc in next dc and in each dc across.

Finish off.

INSTRUCTIONS

Ch 60{72}; being careful **not** to twist ch, join with slip st to form a ring.

Rnd 1 (Right side)**:** Ch 3 **(counts as first dc)**, dc in next ch and in each ch around; join with slip st to first dc: 60{72} dc.

Rnd 2: Ch 1, sc in same st and in each dc around; join with slip st to first sc.

Rnd 3: Ch 1, sc in same st, ★ ch 5, skip next 3 sc, sc in next sc; repeat from ★ around to last 3 sc, ch 2, skip last 3 sc, dc in first sc to form last ch-5 sp: 15{18} ch-5 sps.

Rnd 4: Ch 1, sc in last ch-5 sp made, 7 dc in next ch-5 sp, sc in next ch-5 sp, ★ ch 5, sc in next ch-5 sp, 7 dc in next ch-5 sp, sc in next ch-5 sp; repeat from ★ around, ch 2, dc in first sc to form last ch-5 sp: 5{6} 7-dc groups and 5{6} ch-5 sps.

Begin working in rows.

Row 1: Ch 1, sc in last ch-5 sp made, ch 1, (dc in next dc, ch 1) 7 times, sc in next ch-5 sp, leave remaining sts unworked: 8 ch-1 sps.

Row 2: Ch 1, **turn**; (sc, ch 2, sc) in each ch-1 sp across, slip st in last sc; finish off.

Owl Magnets

 *Shown on page 21.*

 **EASY**

Finished Size: Approximately 4¼" high x 3¾" wide (11 cm x 9.5 cm)

SHOPPING LIST

Yarn (Medium Weight) [4]

- ☐ Dk Rose or Green - 20 yards (18.5 meters)
- ☐ White - 12 yards (11 meters)
- ☐ Black - 7 yards (6.5 meters)
- ☐ Orange or Lt Teal - 6 yards (5.5 meters)
- ☐ Pink or Dk Green - 3 yards (2.5 meters)
- ☐ Rose or Blue - 3 yards (2.5 meters)

Crochet Hook

- ☐ Size H (5 mm)

Additional Supplies

- ☐ Polyester fiberfill
- ☐ Self-adhesive magnetic strip - 2

—— STITCH GUIDE ——

 TREBLE CROCHET
(abbreviated tr)

YO twice, insert hook in st indicated, YO and pull up a loop (4 loops on hook), (YO and draw through 2 loops on hook) 3 times.

COLOR SEQUENCE

Asleep Owl - Rose, Dk Rose, Orange, Pink, and Dk Rose.

Awake Owl - Green, Blue, Lt Teal, Dk Green, and Green.

19

INSTRUCTIONS

Body (Make 2)

Rnd 1 (Right side)**:** With first color and  using an adjustable loop *(Figs. 1a-d, page 44)*, work 10 sc in ring; join with slip st to first sc  changing to next color *(Fig. 6b, page 46)*.

Note: Loop a short piece of yarn around any stitch to mark Rnd 1 as **right** side.

Rnd 2: Ch 1, sc in same st, ch 1, (sc in next sc, ch 1) around; join with slip st to first sc changing to next color: 10 sc and 10 ch-1 sps.

Rnd 3: (Slip st, ch 1, sc) in next ch-1 sp, ch 1, (2 sc in next ch-1 sp, ch 1) around, sc in same sp as first sc; join with slip st to first sc changing to next color: 20 sc and 10 ch-1 sps.

Rnd 4: (Slip st, ch 1, 3 sc) in next ch-1 sp, ch 1, (3 sc in next ch-1 sp, ch 1) around; join with slip st to first sc changing to next color: 30 sc and 10 ch-1 sps.

Rnd 5: Ch 1, sc in same st and in next 2 sc, 2 sc in next ch-1 sp, (sc in next 3 sc, 2 sc in next ch-1 sp) around; join with slip st to first sc: 50 sc.

Rnd 6: Ch 1, sc in same st and in each sc around to last 9 sc, hdc in next sc, (dc, tr, dc) in next sc, hdc in next sc, sc in next 3 sc, hdc in next sc, (dc, tr, dc) in next sc, hdc in last sc; join with slip st to first sc, finish off.

Eye (Make 2)

Rnd 1: Using an adjustable loop and White, work 10 sc in ring; join with slip st to first sc.

Rnd 2: Ch 1, 2 sc in same st and in each sc around; join with slip st to first sc, finish off leaving a long end for sewing.

Using photo as a guide:
With Black,  embroider open eyes' pupils using satin stitch or closed eyes using straight stitch *(see Embroidery Stitches, page 47)*.

Sew eyes to one Body.

Using satin stitch and Orange, embroider a beak between the eyes.

Joining Rnd: With **wrong** sides together, and working through **both** loops of each st on **both** pieces, join Rose for the Asleep Owl or Green for the Awake Owl with slip st in any st; slip st in each st around, stuffing lightly with fiberfill before closing; join with slip st to joining slip st, finish off.

Attach magnetic strip to back.

Pencil Topper

◼◼☐▷ **EASY**

INSTRUCTIONS

Ch 4; join with slip st to form a ring.

Rnd 1: Ch 1, 4 sc in ring; join with slip st to 🎥 Back Loop Only of first sc *(Fig. 2, page 45)*.

Rnds 2 and 3: Ch 1, working in Back Loops Only, sc in each sc around; join with slip st to first sc.

Rnd 4: Ch 1, sc in Back Loop Only of each sc around; join with slip st to **both** loops of first sc.

Rnd 5: Ch 3, (3 dc, ch 3, slip st) in same st, (slip st, ch 3, 3 dc, ch 3, slip st) in next sc and in each sc around; join with slip st to joining slip st, finish off.

Butterfly Barrette

EASY

SHOPPING LIST

Yarn (Medium Weight) 📍4
- ☐ Purple - 7 yards (6.5 meters)
- ☐ Pink - 7 yards (6.5 meters)
- ☐ Green - 3 yards (2.5 meters)

Crochet Hook
- ☐ Size H (5 mm)

Additional Supplies
- ☐ Yarn needle
- ☐ Barrette - 2" (5 cm) long

INSTRUCTIONS

With Green, ch 5; join with slip st to form a ring.

Note: Loop a short piece of yarn around any stitch to mark Rnd 1 as **right** side.

Rnd 1 (Right side)**:** Ch 3 **(counts as first dc, now and throughout)**, 2 dc in ring, ch 5, (3 dc in ring, ch 5) 3 times; join with slip st to first dc, finish off: 12 dc and 4 ch-5 sps.

Rnd 2: With **right** side facing, join Purple with slip st in last ch of any ch-5; ch 3, ★ † 2 dc in next dc, dc in next dc, 2 dc in next dc, dc in next ch, ch 3, 🎥 working **around** ch-5 *(Fig. 5, page 46)*, sc in ring,

ch 3 †, dc in last ch of same ch-5; repeat from ★ 2 times **more**, then repeat from † to † once; join with slip st to first dc, finish off leaving a long end for sewing: 32 sts and 8 ch-3 sps.

Wing: With **right** side facing, join Pink with slip st in last sc made; † ch 4, dc in next dc, 2 dc in each of next 5 dc, dc in next dc, ch 4 †, sc in next sc, repeat from † to † once, slip st in next sc, leave remaining sts unworked; finish off.

Sew barrette to **wrong** side of Butterfly.

Lip Balm Cover

◼◼▭▭ **EASY**

Size: Fits most lip balm tubes

SHOPPING LIST

Yarn (Medium Weight) **4**
☐ 12 yards (11 meters)

Crochet Hook
☐ Size H (5 mm)

Additional Supplies
☐ Yarn needle

INSTRUCTIONS
Body

Rnd 1: Using an adjustable loop *(Figs. 1a-d, page 44)*, work 8 sc in ring; do **not** join, place marker to indicate beginning of rnd *(see Markers, page 43)*.

Rnds 2-7: Working in Back Loops Only *(Fig. 2, page 45)*, sc in each sc around.

Rnd 8: Sc in Back Loops Only of each sc around; slip st in **both** loops of next sc, finish off.

Top

Work same as Body through Rnd 3, at end of Rnd 3; slip st in **both** loops of next sc, finish off leaving a long end for sewing.

Flower

Rnd 1: Using an adjustable loop, work 15 sc in ring; join with slip st to first sc.

Rnd 2: Ch 5, (slip st in next sc, ch 5) around; join with slip st to joining slip st, finish off leaving a long end for sewing.

Sew 3 sc of last rnd of Top and Body together; then sew Flower to side of Top.

Coaster

 EASY

Finished Size: 5½" (14 cm) square

GAUGE INFORMATION

Gauge Swatch: 2½" (6.25 cm) square

Work same as Rnds 1 and 2, page 30:

24 hdc and 8 sps.

INSTRUCTIONS

With Gold, ch 4; join with slip st to form a ring.

Rnd 1 (Right side)**:** Ch 3 (**counts as first hdc plus ch 1**), (3 hdc in ring, ch 1) 3 times, 2 hdc in ring; join with slip st to first hdc: 12 hdc and 4 ch-1 sps.

Note: Loop a short piece of yarn around any stitch to mark Rnd 1 as **right** side.

Rnd 2: Slip st in next ch-1 sp, ch 2 (**counts as first hdc, now and throughout**), (2 hdc, ch 2, 3 hdc) in same sp, ch 1, ★ (3 hdc, ch 2, 3 hdc) in next ch-1 sp, ch 1; repeat from ★ 2 times **more**; join with slip st to first hdc, finish off: 24 hdc and 8 sps.

Rnd 3: With **right** side facing, join Green with slip st in any corner ch-2 sp; ch 2, (2 hdc, ch 2, 3 hdc) in same sp, ch 1, 3 hdc in next ch-1 sp, ch 1, ★ (3 hdc, ch 2, 3 hdc) in next corner ch-2 sp, ch 1, 3 hdc in next ch-1 sp, ch 1; repeat from ★ 2 times **more**; join with slip st to first hdc, finish off: 36 hdc and 12 sps.

Rnd 4: With **right** side facing, join Pink with slip st in any corner ch-2 sp; ch 2, (2 hdc, ch 2, 3 hdc) in same sp, ch 1, (3 hdc in next ch-1 sp, ch 1) twice, ★ (3 hdc, ch 2, 3 hdc) in next corner ch-2 sp, ch 1, (3 hdc in next ch-1 sp, ch 1) twice; repeat from ★ 2 times **more**; join with slip st to first hdc: 48 hdc and 16 sps.

Rnd 5: Slip st in next 2 hdc, ch 2, 4 hdc in same st, sc in next ch-2 sp, skip next 2 hdc, ★ 5 hdc in next hdc, sc in next sp, skip next 2 sts; repeat from ★ around; join with slip st to first hdc, finish off.

 Slippers

Shown on page 33.

 **EASY**

SHOPPING LIST

Yarn (Medium Weight)

[7 ounces, 364 yards
(198 grams, 333 meters)
per skein]:

☐ Blue - 1 skein

☐ Red - 20 yards (18.5 meters)

Crochet Hook

☐ Size H (5 mm)
or size needed for gauge

Additional Supplies

☐ ⁷/₈" (22 mm) Buttons - 2

☐ Sewing needle & matching thread

SIZE INFORMATION

Size: Child {Adult}

Size Note: We have printed
the instructions for the sizes in
different colors to make it easier
for you to find:

• Child Size in Blue

• Adult Size in Green

Instructions in Black apply to both
sizes.

GAUGE INFORMATION

15 dc and 9 rows = 4" (10 cm)

Gauge Swatch:

2½" (6.25 cm) diameter
Work same as Toe Rnds 1-3,
page 34: 24 dc.

STITCH GUIDE

SINGLE CROCHET TOGETHER *(abbreviated sc2tog)* (uses 2 sc)
Pull up a loop in marked sc and in next sc, YO and draw through all 3 loops on hook **(counts as one sc)**.

REVERSE SINGLE CROCHET *(abbreviated reverse sc)*
Working from **left** to **right**, ★ insert hook in st to right of hook *(Fig. A)*, YO and draw through, under and to left of loop on hook (2 loops on hook) *(Fig. B)*, YO and draw through both loops on hook *(Fig. C) (reverse sc made, Fig. D)*; repeat from ★ around.

Fig. A

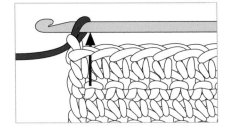

Fig. B

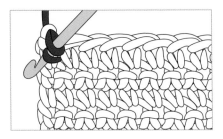

Fig. C

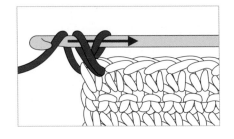

Fig. D

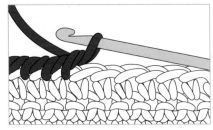

INSTRUCTIONS
Toe

Rnd 1 (Right side)**:** With Blue and  using an adjustable loop *(Figs. 1a-d, page 44)*, ch 2 **(beginning ch-2 does not count as a st, now and throughout)**, work 8 dc in ring; join with slip st to top of beginning ch-2.

Note: Loop a short piece of yarn around any stitch to mark Rnd 1 as **right** side.

Rnd 2: Ch 2, 2 dc in first dc and in each dc around; join with slip st to top of beginning ch-2: 16 dc.

Rnd 3: Ch 2, dc in first dc, 2 dc in next dc, (dc in next dc, 2 dc in next dc) around; join with slip st to top of beginning ch-2: 24 dc.

Rnd 4: Ch 2, dc in first 2 dc, 2 dc in next dc, (dc in next 2 dc, 2 dc in next dc) around; join with slip st to top of beginning ch-2: 32 dc.

Adult Size Only

Rnd 5: Ch 2, dc in first 3 dc, 2 dc in next dc, (dc in next 3 dc, 2 dc in next dc) around; join with slip st to top of beginning ch-2: 40 dc.

Both Sizes

Rnd 5{6}: Ch 2, dc in first dc and in each dc around; join with slip st to top of beginning ch-2.

Foot

Begin working in rows.

Row 1: Ch 2, dc in first 23{31} dc, leave remaining 9 dc unworked.

Row 2: Ch 2, turn; dc in first dc and in each dc across.

Repeat Row 2 until Foot measures desired length, do **not** finish off.

Heel Seam: Fold last row with **right** side together, ch 1; 🎥 slip st in inside loops of each st across; finish off.

EDGING

Rnd 1: With **right** side facing, 🎥 join Blue with sc in seam *(see Joining With Sc, page 43)*; 2 sc in end of each row across to Row 1, sc in end of Row 1, pull up a loop in same row and in same st on Toe as last dc on Row 1, YO and draw through all 3 loops on hook **(counts as one sc)**, place marker in sc just made, sc in next 9 dc, pull up a loop in top of beginning ch-2 on Toe and in end of Row 1 on Foot, YO and draw through all 3 loops on hook **(counts as one sc)**, place marker in sc just made, sc in end of same row, 2 sc in end of each row across; join with slip st to first sc, finish off.

Rnd 2: With **right** side facing, join Red with sc in first sc; (sc in each sc around to marked sc, sc2tog) twice, sc in each sc around; join with slip st to first sc.

Rnd 3 - Left Slipper: Ch 1, working from **left** to **right**, work reverse sc in each sc around to within 4 sc of first decrease; ch 25 (strap), work reverse sc in next sc and in each sc around; join with slip st to first st, finish off.

Rnd 3 - Right Slipper: Ch 1, working from **left** to **right**, work reverse sc in each sc around to 4 sc **after** second decrease, ch 25 (strap), work reverse sc in next sc and in each sc around; join with slip st to first st, finish off.

Sew a button to side of each Slipper opposite strap.

❋ ❋ ❋ Can Cozy ❋ ❋ ❋

 **EASY**

Finished Size: Fits most drink cans

SHOPPING LIST

Yarn (Medium Weight) 🧶 **MEDIUM 4**
- ☐ Dk Green - 25 yards (23 meters)
- ☐ Blue - 5 yards (4.5 meters)
- ☐ Green - 5 yards (4.5 meters)
- ☐ Lime - 3 yards (2.5 meters)
- ☐ White - small amount

Crochet Hook
- ☐ Size H (5 mm)

Additional Supplies
- ☐ Yarn needle

INSTRUCTIONS

Rnd 1 (Right side)**:** With Dk Green and 🎥 using an adjustable loop *(Figs. 1a-d, page 44)*, work 5 sc in ring; join with slip st to first sc.

Note: Loop a short piece of yarn around any stitch to mark Rnd 1 as **right** side.

Rnd 2: Ch 1, 2 sc in each sc around; join with slip st to first sc: 10 sc.

Rnd 3: Ch 1, 2 sc in same st, sc in next sc, (2 sc in next sc, sc in next sc) around; join with slip st to first sc: 15 sc.

Rnd 4: Ch 1, 2 sc in same st, sc in next 2 sc, (2 sc in next sc, sc in next 2 sc) around; join with slip st to first sc: 20 sc.

Rnd 5: Ch 1, 2 sc in same st, sc in next 3 sc, (2 sc in next sc, sc in next 3 sc) around; join with slip st to first sc: 25 sc.

Rnd 6: Ch 1, 2 sc in same st, sc in next 4 sc, (2 sc in next sc, sc in next 4 sc) around; join with slip st to first sc: 30 sc.

Rnds 7-12: Ch 1, sc in each sc around; join with slip st to first sc.

Rnd 13: Ch 1, sc in each sc around; join with slip st to first sc 📹 changing to Blue *(Fig. 6b, page 46)*.

Rnd 14: Ch 1, sc in each sc around; join with slip st to first sc.

Rnd 15: Ch 1, sc in each sc around; join with slip st to first sc changing to Green.

Rnd 16: Ch 1, sc in each sc around; join with slip st to first sc.

Rnd 17: Ch 1, sc in each sc around; join with slip st to first sc changing to Lime.

Rnd 18: Ch 1, sc in each sc around; join with slip st to first sc changing to Dk Green.

Rnds 19 and 20: Ch 1, sc in each sc around; join with slip st to first sc.

Finish off.

Stripe: Make a slip knot with White. With **right** side facing, holding working yarn and slip knot on **wrong** side of piece, insert hook in any sc on Rnd 19 and 📹 pull loop of slip knot through st; slip st in each sc around; join with slip st to first slip st, finish off.

Fingerless Mitts

Shown on page 41.

  EASY

Finished Size: 7" long x 7¼" circumference (17.75 cm x 18.5 cm)

SHOPPING LIST

Yarn (Medium Weight)

☐ Green - 25 yards (23 meters)

☐ Lt Blue - 15 yards (13.5 meters)

☐ Gold - 15 yards (13.5 meters)

☐ Pink - 15 yards (13.5 meters)

☐ Blue - 15 yards (13.5 meters)

☐ Off-White - 15 yards
   (13.5 meters)

Crochet Hook

☐ Size H (5 mm)

or size needed for gauge

Additional Supplies

☐ Yarn needle

GAUGE INFORMATION

In pattern,

   (sc, ch 3, Cluster, ch 1)

   3 times = 3½" (9 cm);

   8 rows = 4½" (11.5 cm)

Gauge Swatch: 7"w x 2¼"h

   (17.75 cm x 5.75 cm)

Work same as Mitt, page 40,

through Row 4: 13 sts and 12 sps.

— STITCH GUIDE —

🎥 BEGINNING CLUSTER

(uses 2 chs)

Ch 4, turn; YO, insert hook in third ch from hook, YO and pull up a loop, YO and draw through 2 loops on hook, YO, insert hook in last ch, YO and pull up a loop, YO and draw through 2 loops on hook, YO and draw through all 3 loops on hook.

🎥 CLUSTER

(uses one st or sp)

★ YO, insert hook in st or sp indicated, YO and pull up a loop, YO and draw through 2 loops on hook; repeat from ★ once **more**, YO and draw through all 3 loops on hook.

🎥 ENDING CLUSTER

(uses last sp and last sc)

★ YO, insert hook in last sp, YO and pull up a loop, YO and draw through 2 loops on hook; repeat from ★ once **more**, insert hook in last sc, YO and pull up a loop, YO and draw through all 4 loops on hook.

STRIPE SEQUENCE

One row **each**: Green ★ Lt Blue, Gold, Pink, Blue, Off-White, Green; repeat from ★ once **more**.

INSTRUCTIONS

Mitt (Make 2)

With Green, ch 26.

Row 1 (Right side): (Sc, ch 3, Cluster) in second ch from hook, ch 1, ★ skip next 3 chs, (sc, ch 3, Cluster) in next ch, ch 1; repeat from ★ across to last 4 chs, skip next 3 chs, sc in last ch 🎥 changing to Lt Blue (*Fig. 6a, page 46*): 13 sts and 12 sps.

Note: Loop a short piece of yarn around any stitch to mark Row 1 as **right** side.

Row 2: Work Beginning Cluster, ch 1, ★ (sc, ch 3, Cluster) in next ch-3 sp, ch 1; repeat from ★ 4 times **more**, sc in last sp, ch 2, work Ending Cluster changing to next color.

Row 3: Ch 1, turn; sc in top of Ending Cluster, ch 2, work Cluster in next ch-2 sp, ch 1, ★ (sc, ch 3, Cluster) in next ch-3 sp, ch 1; repeat from ★ across, sc in top of Beginning Cluster changing to next color.

Rows 4-13: Repeat Rows 2 and 3, 5 times; at end of Row 13, do not change color; finish off.

With **wrong** side facing, sew ends of rows together from Row 1 through Row 3. Skip next 3 rows for thumb opening and sew Row 7 through Row 13 together.

❋ ❋ ❋ GENERAL ❋ ❋ ❋
INSTRUCTIONS

ABBREVIATIONS

BPsc	Back Post single crochet(s)
ch(s)	chain(s)
cm	centimeters
dc	double crochet(s)
hdc	half double crochet(s)
mm	millimeters
Rnd(s)	Round(s)
sc	single crochet(s)
sc2tog	single crochet 2 together
sp(s)	space(s)
st(s)	stitch(es)
tr	treble crochet(s)
YO	yarn over

SYMBOLS & TERMS

★ — work instructions following ★ as many **more** times as indicated in addition to the first time.

† to † — work all instructions from first † to second † **as many** times as specified.

( ) or **[ ]** — work enclosed instructions as many times as specified by the number immediately following **or** work all enclosed instructions in the stitch or space indicated **or** contains explanatory remarks.

colon (:) — the number(s) given after a colon at the end of a row or round denote(s) the number of stitches or spaces you should have on that row or round.

CROCHET TERMINOLOGY		
UNITED STATES		INTERNATIONAL
slip stitch (slip st)	=	single crochet (sc)
single crochet (sc)	=	double crochet (dc)
half double crochet (hdc)	=	half treble crochet (htr)
double crochet (dc)	=	treble crochet(tr)
treble crochet (tr)	=	double treble crochet (dtr)
double treble crochet (dtr)	=	triple treble crochet (ttr)
triple treble crochet (tr tr)	=	quadruple treble crochet (qtr)
skip	=	miss

GAUGE

Exact gauge is **essential** for proper size. Before beginning your project, make the sample swatch given in the individual instructions in the yarn and hook specified. After completing the swatch, measure it, counting your stitches and rows/rounds carefully. If your swatch is larger or smaller than specified, **make another, changing hook size to get the correct gauge.** Keep trying until you find the size hook that will give you the specified gauge.

MARKERS

Markers are used to help distinguish the beginning of each round being worked. Place a 2" (5 cm) scrap piece of yarn before the first stitch of each round, moving marker after each round is complete.

JOINING WITH SC

When instructed to join with sc, begin with a slip knot on hook. Insert hook in stitch or space indicated, YO and pull up a loop, YO and draw through both loops on hook.

CROCHET HOOKS															
U.S.	B-1	C-2	D-3	E-4	F-5	G-6	H-8	I-9	J-10	K-10½	L-11	M/N-13	N/P-15	P/Q	Q	S
Metric - mm	2.25	2.75	3.25	3.5	3.75	4	5	5.5	6	6.5	8	9	10	15	16	19

◖☐☐☐ BEGINNER	Projects for first-time crocheters using basic stitches. Minimal shaping.
◖◖☐☐ EASY	Projects using yarn with basic stitches, repetitive stitch patterns, simple color changes, and simple shaping and finishing.
◖◖◖☐ INTERMEDIATE	Projects using a variety of techniques, such as basic lace patterns or color patterns, mid-level shaping and finishing.
◖◖◖◖ EXPERIENCED	Projects with intricate stitch patterns, techniques and dimension, such as non-repeating patterns, multi-color techniques, fine threads, small hooks, detailed shaping and refined finishing.

ADJUSTABLE LOOP

Wind yarn around two fingers to form a ring *(Fig. 1a)*. Slide yarn off fingers and grasp the strands at the top of the ring *(Fig. 1b)*. Insert hook from **front** to **back** into the ring, pull up a loop, YO and draw through loop on hook to lock ring *(Fig. 1c)* (st made does **not** count as a beginning ch). Working around **both** strands, follow instructions to work sts in the ring, then pull yarn tail to close *(Fig. 1d)*.

Fig. 1a

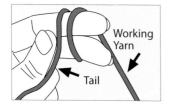

Fig. 1b

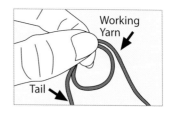

Fig. 1b

Fig. 1c

BACK LOOP ONLY

Work only in loop(s) indicated by arrow *(Fig. 2)*.

POST STITCH

Work around the post of the stitch indicated, inserting the hook in the direction of the arrow *(Fig. 3)*.

Fig. 2

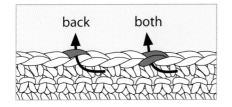

back   both

Fig. 3

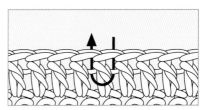

Yarn Weight Symbol & Names	LACE ⓪	SUPER FINE ①	FINE ②	LIGHT ③	MEDIUM ④	BULKY ⑤	SUPER BULKY ⑥
Type of Yarns in Category	Fingering, 10-count crochet thread	Sock, Fingering Baby	Sport, Baby	DK, Light Worsted	Worsted, Afghan, Aran	Chunky, Craft, Rug	Bulky, Roving
Crochet Gauge* Ranges in Single Crochet to 4" (10 cm)	32-42 double crochets**	21-32 sts	16-20 sts	12-17 sts	11-14 sts	8-11 sts	5-9 sts
Advised Hook Size Range	Steel*** 6,7,8 Regular hook B-1	B-1 to E-4	E-4 to 7	7 to I-9	I-9 to K-10.5	K-10.5 to M-13	M-13 and larger

*GUIDELINES ONLY: The chart above reflects the most commonly used gauges and hook sizes for specific yarn categories.

** Lace weight yarns are usually crocheted on larger-size hooks to create lacy openwork patterns. Accordingly, a gauge range is difficult to determine. Always follow the gauge stated in your pattern.

*** Steel crochet hooks are sized differently from regular hooks–the higher the number the smaller the hook, which is the reverse of regular hook sizing.

WORKING IN SPACE BEFORE A STITCH

When instructed to work in space **before** a stitch or in spaces **between** stitches, insert hook in space indicated by arrow *(Fig. 4)*.

Fig. 4

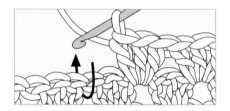

WORKING AROUND A CHAIN

Work in stitch or space indicated, inserting hook in direction of arrow *(Fig. 5)*.

Fig. 5

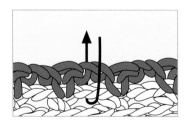

CHANGING COLORS

To change colors at the end of a row, work the last stitch to within one step of completion, hook new yarn *(Fig. 6a)* and draw through all loops on hook.

Fig. 6a

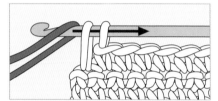

To change colors while joining with slip st, drop yarn, insert hook in first st *(Fig. 6b)*, YO and draw through st **and** loop on hook. Cut old yarn, unless otherwise instructed.

Fig. 6b

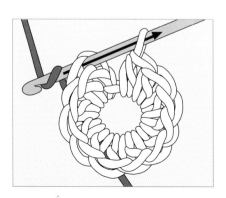

WHIPSTITCH

With **wrong** side together, sew through both edges once to secure the beginning of the seam, leaving an ample yarn end to weave in later. Insert the needle from **front** to **back** through **both** loops of stitches on **both** edges *(Fig. 7)*. Bring the needle around and insert it from **front** to **back** through next loops of both edges. Continue in this manner across, keeping the sewing yarn fairly loose.

Fig. 7

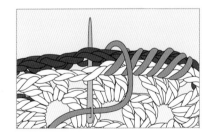

EMBROIDERY STITCHES
Satin Stitch

Satin stitch is a series of straight stitches worked side by side so they touch. Come up at odd numbers and go down at even numbers *(Fig. 8)*.

Fig. 8

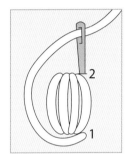

Straight Stitch

Straight stitch is just what the name implies, a single, straight stitch. Come up at 1 and go down at 2 *(Fig. 9)*.

Fig. 9

YARN INFORMATION

Each project in this book was made using Medium Weight Yarn, either Red Heart® Super Saver or Red Heart® With Love. Any brand of Medium Weight Yarn may be used. It is best to refer to the yardage/meters when determining how many balls or skeins to purchase. Remember, to arrive at the finished size, it is the GAUGE/TENSION that is important, not the brand of yarn.

We have made every effort to ensure that these instructions are accurate and complete. We cannot, however, be responsible for human error, typographical mistakes, or variations in individual work.

Production Team: Writer/Instructional Editor - Sarah J. Green; Editorial Writer - Susan Frantz Wiles; Graphic Artist - Becca Snider Tally; Senior Graphic Artist - Lora Puls; Photo Stylist - Sondra Daniel; and Photographer - Ken West.